The Stoic Father - Cultivating Core
Virtues Within Your Family

The Stoic Father - Cultivating Core Virtues Within Your Family

Phillip Deam

Contents

Introduction
Chapter 1: The Virtuous parent
Chapter 2: Balanced Disapline
Chapter 3: Emotional Intelligence in Children
Chapter 4: Building Resilliance
Chapter 5: Family Values and Virtues
Chapter 6: Virtuous Conflict Resolution
Chapter 7: Cultivating Grattitude
Final Thoughts

Introduction

As I sit down to reflect on my journey as a father of three young children, I am struck by the beautiful chaos that fills our home. Each day begins with the energetic laughter of my little ones, their boundless curiosity a constant reminder of the innocence and wonder of childhood. Yet, intertwined with this joy are the challenges that come with parenthood, especially as we navigate the health issues faced by our eldest, a spirited six-year-old who has taught me more about resilience than I ever expected to learn.

The balancing act of work and family life often feels like a highwire performance. I find myself constantly shifting priorities, racing against the clock to meet deadlines while ensuring that my children feel loved and supported. The demands can be overwhelming, and there are days when the weight of it all feels particularly heavy. But in the midst of this whirlwind, I have discovered the principles of Stoicism, which have become my guiding light.

Stoicism has taught me the importance of focusing on what truly matters. It has encouraged me to embrace the present moment, to find strength in adversity, and to cultivate gratitude even on the toughest days. When faced with the uncertainties surrounding my eldest's health, I have learned to channel my energy into what I can control: my reactions, my mindset, and my love for my children. This philosophy has allowed me to approach challenges with clarity, turning obstacles into opportunities for growth.

As I reflect on this journey, I am reminded that parenthood is not just about managing the day-to-day chaos. It is about nurturing our children's spirits, instilling in them values that will carry them through life, and finding joy in the simple moments we share. Each day, I strive to be the father they need, using the lessons of Stoicism to guide me in focusing on love, patience, and understanding.

This book is a testament to the struggles and triumphs of fatherhood, a journey that is as rewarding as it is challenging. It is my hope that my experiences resonate with other parents facing their own battles, and that the principles I've learned can inspire a deeper connection to what truly matters in our lives.

One

The Virtuous Parent

"Man is not worried by real problems so much as by his imagined troubles." - Epictetus

The virtuous parent embodies the principles of Stoicism, understanding that true challenges are often not the external circumstances but the internal narratives we construct. Epictetus reminds us that it is not the actual trials of life that disturb our peace, but rather our perceptions and fears surrounding them. A virtuous parent recognizes this distinction and seeks to cultivate a mindset grounded in reason, virtue, and acceptance.

Parents who embody the Stoic principle of acceptance. They acknowledge that life will present inevitable difficulties—sleepless nights, disappointments, and the unpredictability of a child's growth. Yet, instead of being paralyzed by worry, they cultivate a mindset that welcomes these experiences as opportunities for growth and learning. By accepting the transient nature of life, they teach their children to navigate their own challenges with grace and fortitude.

Guided by the teachings of Stoicism, we understand that the essence of parenting lies not in the avoidance of problems but in the development of virtue in the face of them. By cultivating wisdom, courage, justice, and temperance, they create a legacy that transcends imagined troubles, fostering a home built on the firm ground of Stoic principles. Thus, they prepare their children not only to face the world but to contribute to it with integrity and strength.

The essence of human anxiety and the nature of our perception of it are encapsulated by the Stoic philosopher Epictetus. He suggests that most of our distress does not come from real events or problems—they're more or less like the straw men that philosophers have long held up for refutation—but from our thoughts about these events and challenges. This perception closely harmonizes with Stoic teachings, which hold that the proper distinction between what is and is not within our control is fundamental to a life well-lived. "If you want to be a Stoic," an instructor at the Stoic Week online course put it, "you have to get this distinction."

The way of the Stoics is to not let the storms of life sweep over them. Instead, they wait them out with courage and fortitude. Life can't be 100 percent good; we are bound to encounter some difficulties. Even the most fortunate persons can't avoid setbacks and failures altogether. So, next time you think of using your imagination to create a fantastical scenario, which is what we usually do when we worry about the future, try doing the opposite and imagine something bad happening. But don't stop there. Go on and try to visualize how you would deal with it, how you could carry on with your life as best as you can in the face of whatever-it-is that you imagined.

In terms of psychology, it is about cognitive distortions and the propensity to catastrophize. Cognitive-behavioral therapy (CBT) tackles these patterns, teaching folks to question and recast their thoughts. It helps us see that many of our anxieties are, in fact, projections. This is consistent with what the Stoics advocate: for rational analysis and self-reflection as a way of preventing (or at least, helping us manage) emotional meltdowns. On the surface, all this may seem quite mundane. After all, we all too often have flying monkeys in our heads, telling us we're toast when, in fact, we're not.

In addition, Epictetus underscores the human inclination to fabricate stories about our experiences. Both Stoicism and contemporary psychology direct us to look at these so-called life events and to appraise their true significance. Are they really life-altering events, or are we just putting our usual spin on them? From an emotionally healthy standpoint, which both Epictetus and modern psychology would endorse, it's far better to see things as they are, to suss out the narrative fallacies and invest in more plausible alternative storylines.

Fundamentally, the overlap between Stoic philosophy and psychology shows that a lot of human suffering is of our own making. When we are better at controlling our thoughts and the ways we let events "get to us," we are also better at enduring the kinds of unavoidable hardships that life throws our way. We are better at living with those things, in the same way, we are better problem solvers when we are calm and think clearly than when we are anxious and muddled.

Understanding Virtue in Parenting

Grasping the concept of virtue in parenting means identifying the important values that steer family relationships and child-rearing. For the most part, parenting virtues can be boiled down to four ancient ones—prudence, temperance, fortitude, and justice. If parents can internalize these virtues, they have a reliable framework for steering their family through the tumult of life. If the family can embody these virtues, it is almost certain that the children will carry them along to the next generation.

The four main virtues generally specified across different philosophical and ethical systems are:

Prudence: The ability to make sound judgments and decisions based on knowledge, experience, and understanding. It involves discernment and the capacity to see beyond immediate circumstances.

Courage: The strength to confront fear, uncertainty, and challenges. It includes not only physical bravery but also the moral courage to stand up for what is right.

Temperance: The practice of self-control and moderation. It involves balancing desires and impulses, promoting a sense of harmony and restraint in one's actions.

Justice: The commitment to fairness and equity in dealings with others. It emphasizes the importance of giving each person their due and upholding principles of right and wrong in society.

These words were written in his private meditations by Marcus Aurelius, one of the most prominent Stoic philosophers and Roman emperors. Balancing enormous responsibilities and a world of political turmoil, he nonetheless held that real power lies in the mines our own minds. His point was this: It's far better to try to control our perceptions, judgments, and emotional reactions than to work futilely at controlling the events around us.

This quote embodies a core Stoic and philosophical idea: the nature of our personal internal world is of our own making and therefore poorly served by negative thoughts and feelings. From this perspective, it's easy to see why the Stoics would have identified as their "cognitive reframing" the act of recognizing and reshaping thoughts and feelings of a distressing nature, which are in fact poor judgments of the situation we are in. They would have seen this act of reframing as not only improving our internal world but also making it more resilient to the chaos of unpredictable external circumstances.

Applying this idea to parenting has serious ramifications. It makes the art of parenting sound almost superhuman. There are so many predictable and unpredictable events that occur when dealing with children—tantrums, for instance, which seem to be at least as old as the Bible; sibling rivalry, which seems to be universal; and the social pressures of contemporary life. With all of these, one can easily feel overwhelmed.

The Virtuous President

As the 26th President of the United States, Theodore Roosevelt stands tall in American history, not just for his political accomplishments but also for his deep and abiding commitment to the virtues and characters of American life. More than most, he lived a life that combined the public service of politics and the personal service of family, which certainly offers a ripe opportunity to explore the essence of virtuous parenting in the figure of Teddy Roosevelt.

Theodore Roosevelt had six children: Alice, Theodore Jr., Kermit, Ethel, Archibald, and Quentin. They were all much loved. Aeronautics and astronautics, however, were not pioneered only by the Roosevelt family. In fact, the first major "mistake" in the history of human space flight can be traced back to their family tree. Long before NASA, the European Space Agency, or their satellite Hubble, the Roosevelts (among other Americans) were using telescopes to view the heavens.

The grounding of character development in Roosevelt's mind can be traced to his own life experiences. He knew life would not be easy and would throw up many trials and adversities, and he was set upon making sure his children were well equipped to handle any situation that might arise; they were to be developed into tools of navigational kind. In his letters and other personal accounts, he emphasized the virtues of courage, perseverance, and wisdom—traits that he lived by and that defined both his public persona and his private life.

An example of his parenting approach is seen in a letter he wrote to his daughter, Alice. In it, he urged her to deal with tough situations directly and to tackle them with the bravery he wished to impart to her. He always emphasized the kind of faith that led to action rather than just assent. This letter is one of the few glimpses we have of Theodore Roosevelt as a father. In it, he tells Alice she must learn to face difficulties and not flinch when hard tasks are given to her.

The life of Theodore Roosevelt serves as a powerful testament to the cultivation of virtue, particularly in the family, and especially under the relentless demands of public life. Nature, he believed, was a great teacher, and he and his children found many opportunities for learning and for living the values they believed in when they were outdoors. The family had a hard time staying in one place, and thus they often found themselves in the open air. They had to climb mountains and hack their way through forests, always going deeper and deeper not only into the exterior wilds but also into their interior lives, which gave both public and private virtue a chance to blossom.

Roosevelt's parenting illustrates how the four cardinal virtues can play a part in the everyday decisions of a parent. Wisdom guided him as he taught his children important life lessons. Courage inspired him to let them take risks and to learn from their mistakes. Justice marked his treatment of each child; he made sure they all understood the difference between right and wrong, as well as the importance of respecting everyone else. Temperance was reflected in his approach to discipline; he was firm in a loving way that ensured his children felt both secure and challenged.

Ultimately, Theodore Roosevelt bequeathed not just a virtuous paternal legacy but also one of virtuous presidential leadership that offers profound insights into the parenting art. His life and example illustrate that the cultivation of virtue in children is not a passive business, requiring instead active intention, engagement, and love. We turn now to the principles of parenting with virtue, using Roosevelt's legacy as our guide and his life as an example of the kind of value shaping that produces leaders.

The Four Cardinal Virtues

The foundational framework for that virtuous family life, then, is not just made up of four abstract ideals, but of four specific ways to act in a virtuous manner: to act with prudence, to act with temperance, to act with fortitude, and to act with justice. Each of these ways of acting or being affects families in two ways. First, they help families make decisions that are ethically good and right. Second, they help both parents and children develop certain character traits that are good and right.

Prudence is commonly referred to as practical wisdom, and it encourages thoughtful decision-making. Parents can demonstrate this by making acts and choices that show they have considered the consequences of their decisions. This not only sets a powerful example of judgment for children but also literally teaches them what it means to evaluate situations and come to reasonable conclusions. In saying this, of course, every parent's dream is not only to provide a decent living but also to have an enviable role in their children's lives, either as a target of their children's love, admiration, or as a figure whose accomplishments they can point to as the kind of things one should do in life.

Moderation and self-control are what temperance is all about. These are the essential ingredients for maintaining balance in life. When it comes to family, parents can exhibit and encourage temperance by modeling moderation in their own behaviors. They can also foster an environment in which an excess of anything is discouraged. This works well when talking about screen time, how much sugar we eat, and the way we manage our emotions during conflicts. Children are more likely to spring back from life's difficulties if they have been taught the value of not going to extremes and the art of self-regulation.

Courage, or fortitude, in facing difficulties is vital for building resilience in children. Parents can cultivate fortitude in their children by sharing with them stories of their own hard-lived challenges and how they overcame them, thus well-normalizing the experience of struggle. They are also encouraged to face their fears—tiny and tall ones—like trying new physical activities or venturing into (and handling) various social situations with a developing bravado and confidence. A supportive environment where "learning from our mistakes" is held as a pinnacle to reach towards enables a mindset focused on embracing challenges, unyieldingly persevering, and personal growth—part of emotional musculature.

Fairness and equity: The vital family discipline ingredient that is justice, can ensure a balanced approach that supports and reinforces parenting. Justice asks parents to ensure that rules and expectations are applied equally and consistently to all family members, and that consequences for rule infractions are fair and in line with the offense. When family members discuss fairness, either in the context of play or in resolving a conflict, they are practicing an important family habit that is virtually guaranteed to enhance the empathy and respect for others that all family members should cultivate as they develop their individual characters.

The Role of Virtue in Family Dynamics

Family dynamics are profoundly influenced by the cultivation of virtues. When virtues are abundant in a family, there is a serious environment of support and a superabundance of not just healthy, but also nourishing, individuality. When I speak of virtues, the first few that come to my mind are prudence, temperance, fortitude, and justice. These virtues not only shape character in individuals but also help to serve as a collective ethos in families. When parents embody these virtues, when they live them out, they create a culture where the next generations are virtuous not just in private but also, and especially, in public.

A critical aspect of family decision-making and effective conflict resolution is prudence. It enables parents to assess and ponder over a situation for a moment before reacting, which in turn allows them to show their children how to make careful, considered, and foresighted decisions. Children learn from the example of their parents. And when it comes to the interplay of parenting and emotional intelligence, decision-making under conditions of uncertainty is equivalent to "the forward planning involved in parenting." In fact, we might just as well refer to parenting as "the art of forward planning."

The context of discipline and emotional regulation makes temperance, or self-control, essential. Families that practice temperance create an environment in which emotions are managed constructively. That reduces the likelihood of conflict and fosters a sense of stability. Balanced discipline techniques—rooted in justice and temperance—allow parents to enforce rules while also demonstrating empathy and fairness. This approach nurtures moderation and imparts the tools of self-regulation necessary for children to manage the ups and downs of life without resorting to extreme behaviors.

Courage and resilience—what one might call the "virtue of getting back up"—constitute the foundation of fortitude. In a family life, fortitude means more than simply encouragement when children face difficult tasks. Parents are in a partnership with their children that takes pathos and ethos. Pathos plays out through the child's experience of the parent's failed attempts and eventual successes at the tasks of life. Ethos is established when children see their parents tackle life with a determinate resilience that always aims for a positive end. Then it is virtuous encouragement that propels the child toward future obstacles that might be encounters instead of roadblocks.

Ultimately, the integration of key virtues into the core of family values creates a relished relationship. A shared sense of mission—virtue-centered and family culture in my estimation—enhances the family dynamic. It strengthens familial affection. This is a good thing, and I urge you to do it. It isn't hard. In fact, it may be easier than you think. Start with your family, and build outward. Vertically, your ancestors and descendants enrich the family's virtue-enhanced culture. Horizontally, the same holds for your relatives and those you consider family. Your family is the first moral community you inhabit. Make it a virtuous one.

Two

Balanced Discipline

*"**D**iscipline is the bridge between accomplishment and goals." - Jim Rohn*

"Discipline is the bridge between accomplishment and goals." - Jim Rohn

Balanced discipline is the embodiment of Stoic virtues, serving as the vital link between our aspirations and their realization. In the Stoic framework, discipline transcends simple restraint; it represents a calculated approach to action informed by reason and virtue. This disciplined approach requires us to engage our rational faculties to discern what is truly valuable and worthwhile.

The Stoics teach that self-control is not an act of suppression but an exercise in understanding our desires and impulses. True strength is found in the ability to regulate these urges, ensuring they align with our higher purpose. This self-mastery allows us to navigate the complexities of life with composure and integrity, directing our efforts toward goals that reflect our values.

In the practice of balanced discipline, we learn to harmonize our ambitions with our ethical principles. The Stoic virtues—wisdom, courage, justice, and temperance—serve as guiding beacons. Wisdom enables us to identify the goals that genuinely matter, while courage empowers us to pursue them despite adversity. Justice reminds us to consider the impact of our actions on others, and temperance ensures that our desires do not lead us astray.

As we cultivate these skills, we find that it fosters resilience. The road to accomplishment is often fraught with obstacles, yet a disciplined mind remains steadfast, acknowledging challenges as opportunities for growth. By embracing the Stoic perspective, we understand that our responses to external circumstances are within our control. This realization fortifies our resolve and enhances our ability to remain focused on our objectives.

Moreover, balanced discipline nurtures a sense of purpose. When our actions are guided by Stoic virtues, we align ourselves with a greater narrative, one that transcends transient desires. Each disciplined choice becomes a step toward not only personal success but also the betterment of our character. In this way, we build a legacy of integrity that resonates beyond our individual pursuits.

It is a manifestation of our commitment to living a virtuous life. It is the bridge that connects our lofty ambitions with the concrete realities of our existence. By embodying this principle, we become architects of our destiny, crafting a life defined by purpose, resilience, and unwavering adherence to the Stoic path.

In the pursuit of goals, balanced discipline requires a harmonious blend of courage, wisdom, and temperance. Courage allows us to face challenges head-on, while wisdom guides our decisions, helping us discern which actions align with our values. Temperance, the virtue of moderation, ensures that our pursuit does not lead to excess or distraction, maintaining our focus on what truly matters.

The interplay of these virtues within balanced discipline fosters resilience. Stoics recognize that setbacks are inevitable, yet it is our disciplined response to these setbacks that defines our character. By cultivating a disciplined mind, we fortify ourselves against external chaos and internal turmoil, allowing us to remain steadfast in our commitments.

While balanced discipline nurtures a sense of purpose. It encourages reflection on our goals, prompting us to align them with our moral compass. This alignment ensures that our pursuits are not driven by fleeting desires but by a deeper understanding of what constitutes a virtuous life.

Discipline serves as a continual practice, a commitment to the Stoic path. It invites us to engage consistently in actions that reflect our values, paving the way for a life marked by integrity and fulfillment. In this light, discipline becomes not just a means to an end but a profound expression of our character, bridging the gap between who we are and who we aspire to be.

Balanced discipline serves as the essential framework that connects our aspirations with tangible achievements. It is the resolute adherence to principles that guides us through the tumultuous nature of existence. In the Stoic philosophy, discipline is not merely a tool for productivity; it is a manifestation of virtue, intertwining with wisdom, courage, and justice.

A skill set such as this requires the cultivation of self-control, allowing us to navigate desires and distractions that threaten to derail our progress. It demands that we recognize the impermanent nature of external circumstances and focus instead on our internal responses. By exercising discipline, we embody the Stoic virtue of wisdom, discerning what truly matters and aligning our actions with our values.

The interplay of courage and discipline cannot be overlooked. True discipline often necessitates the bravery to confront discomfort and adversity. It is in these moments of challenge that we must summon our inner strength, persevering in the face of obstacles. This alignment of virtues enhances our ability to remain steadfast in pursuit of our goals, regardless of the trials we encounter.

Justice, too, has a role in balanced discipline. It calls upon us to consider the broader impact of our actions on ourselves and others. A disciplined individual recognizes that their pursuits must not only serve personal ambition but should also contribute to the greater good. In this way, discipline becomes a communal virtue, fostering harmony and shared purpose.

Thus, balanced discipline is not an isolated virtue but a harmonious synthesis of Stoic principles. It empowers us to act with intention, guiding our efforts toward meaningful accomplishments. In embracing this interconnectedness, we cultivate a life of purpose, reflecting the Stoic ideal of living in accordance with nature—both our own and that of the world around us.

There are two key components: structure and commitment. Without these two elements in place, it is hard to see how personal objectives can be achieved. Balanced discipline embodies self-regulation, which is also necessary for the достижение (pronounced dah-stee-ZHEN-ye; Russian for "achieving" or "attainment") of personal freedom. Self-regulation is the path to the Russian verb регрессия (pronounced ree-GRES-see-yah; for "regression" or "backward"). On the contrary, balanced discipline does not have self-regulation at its core. Rather, it embodies the kind of self-regulation that is not a step back but a step toward freedom.

A psychological perspective on balanced discipline reveals it to be self-control and the ability to delay gratification, which are key components of emotional intelligence. A person with emotional intelligence has the cognitive processes that enable them to line up their actions with long-term goals. Balanced discipline yields resilient individuals who possess a growth mindset (i.e., the mindset that allows them to learn from their mistakes).

The interaction between these fields of study illustrates how the fundamental philosophical principles at the core of each discipline can inform the practices of the adjacent discipline. Taking an approach that is balanced and informed by both fields encourages individuals to cultivate the virtues that lead not only to a correct understanding but also to a psychology of right living—an understanding that is more and more hard to come by in our fast-paced and often extreme world.

Defining Balanced Discipline

Discipline that is balanced is a holy component of parenting that is virtuous. It is the parenting that serves as a bridge between the two essential planks of authority and compassion. They recognize the reduced parenting that is necessary for setting safe and secure boundaries while simultaneously nurturing the child's emotional well-being. At its core, balanced discipline is a parenting style that reflects the principles of justice and temperance—ensuring that when misbehavior occurs, the consequences are fair; the consequences are also proportional and aimed at teaching, rather than punishing.

One of the principal facets of even-handed discipline is setting up clear expectations and consistent consequences. Parents play an essential role in this aspect; they provide a model of behaviors that reflect values the family holds, which makes a kind of path for children to walk on when it comes to understanding what's acceptable and what's not. By having a kind of talk with children that covers these bases, parents help their children not only to visualize what's okay and what's not but also to see the kind of walk that leads from one to the other.

Balanced discipline requires emotional intelligence. It is of utmost importance to help children identify and articulate their feelings. This is what leads them to develop the much-needed empathy that allows them to understand others better. But isn't communication just another form of expression? Isn't it just a fancy way of saying "talking with others"? Well, yes and no. Talking with others encompasses a broad range of forms and functions, both verbal and nonverbal. And the effectiveness of our communication is largely dependent on the clarity of our expression.

Another pivotal outcome of balanced discipline is resilience. When children are given consequences, the emphasis needs to be on learning to avoid errors in the future rather than on fear or shame. Parents can (and should) help their children think through and reflect on the experiences that result in a consequence—a kind of "think before you act" in reverse—that also encourages and models good problem-solving skills. These scenarios help children develop a mindset in which they view setbacks as opportunities for growth and some form of personal development.

In the end, balanced discipline is a means of creating a family culture that holds core virtues as paramount. It is not an easy task in today's world, where so many unvirtuous examples are on display, and parenting itself is so often criticized. But with the right tools and the right mindset, any family can use balanced discipline to construct a daily culture that prizes gratitude and respect and holds family members accountable for misunderstanding conflicts with the aim of resolving them. In such a culture, any family can live as a family of virtuous members who serve and respect one another.

− BALANCED DISCIPLINE

Techniques for Fair Disciplinary Methods

The family environment must reflect justice and temperance, especially when it comes to the establishment of disciplinary methods. Parents can reduce the need for punitive measures by setting their children up in advance for positive behavior. What follows are techniques that have worked for others and may work for you as well.

1. Set clear expectations and consequences for behavior.
2. Be sure to communicate the family's values and the rationale behind specific rules.
3. Encourage your children to think critically about the kind of behavior you expect and the kind of behavior that generates consequences.

Another crucial method centers around using restorative discipline instead of punitive measures. This technique emphasizes the importance of understanding the impact of one's behavior on others and of mending relationships over just doling out consequences. Parents can have teetering discussions that elicit important feelings from children and also make them think about the impact of their acts on others. This not only helps parents readjust the emotional intelligence of their kids back to a healthy level but also serves as the first step toward conflict resolution. And "mending injuries" must happen, for both sides, if we are to have any family semblance to a well-functioning community.

Another effective strategy for maintaining fair disciplinary methods is to incorporate positive reinforcement. Recognizing and rewarding desirable behaviors makes it more likely that children will repeat those actions in the future. There are various ways to reinforce a child's positive behavior—verbal praise, small rewards, and the granting of special privileges, to name a few. A child knows she's done something right that deserves recognition and a little reward when she comes into a room full of family members who are congratulating her for what? "Oh, nothing much—except for wearing that shirt with a virtue printed on it. We just thought you'd really appreciate our coming together to honor your 'mirror moment.'"

It is also very important to show exemplary behavior in everyday situations. Children learn by watching their parents, and so it is vital to demonstrate prudence, temperance, fortitude, and justice in daily interactions. Parents should handle conflicts, setbacks, and other challenges with grace and integrity, showing the kinds of behaviors that the difficult situations they're in might tempt them to not exhibit. And when parents are modeling these virtues, they should be thinking of the children they're going to discipline as their contextually relevant audience.

In closing, the ability to hold an open dialogue about feelings and life experiences can significantly enhance the effectiveness of disciplinary methods. Regularly scheduled family meetings or one-on-one powwows allow children to share their thoughts and concerns. This act alone promotes a higher emotional intelligence within the family. If members feel comfortable sharing in a meeting, they are more likely to share concerns that could impact family life in the future. When family members feel heard, they are more likely to respect the rules. Also, children are using these meetings as practice for future discussions where they need to share their side of the story. Hearing a child's side of the story can go a long way toward helping the authoritative figure understand what is respectful and unfair.

21 — BALANCED DISCIPLINE

Dr. Maria Montessori

A brilliant figure shines in the world of education. A figure whose influence pervades the very essence of schools—from kindergartens to universities. Of course, this figure is not a mere silhouette. It stands out in clear relief, as precocious and enduring as the figures on the famous Italian frescoes that line the walls of Renaissance palaces. This is Maria Montessori. Teachers and children all over the world are her grateful disciples. And now, you are one, too, if you have only read this far.

The principle of freedom within boundaries is what underlies the Montessori concept of education. Children flourish, she believed, when they are given the autonomy to make choices, especially if those choices are made within a context that is not only well-structured but also intelligently so. This is a form of discipline, but one that arises from an almost reverential stance toward the child's autonomy and dignity. Montessori almost never spoke of education in and of itself, but rather in terms of the wonderful path of development that the child is invited to take, a development that is richly self-directed at almost every turn.

Maria's vision of discipline is centered on the concept of providing children with positive guidance. It might seem obvious that children need to be guided positively, but the world of child rearing is full of methods that give children the opposite impression. For example, punishment might seem like a method of guiding a child to do the right thing, but it often results in a child thinking in terms of what not to do rather than in terms of what to do. Montessori's method results in a child not feeling capable.

1. Comprehend the child's wrongful behavior within the framework of their growth.

2. Assist the child in understanding the connection between their action and the result, particularly if the result was not what they intended or expected and to consider their choice's impact on others. It is not about making children feel as though they are admitting to something in a way that conveys guilt, but rather, it is about encouraging the child to take ownership of their actions and consider the result of those actions in a reflective way.

Maria also emphasized the importance of nurturing a feeling of responsibility for both oneself and one's environment in children. Giving children the responsibility of caring for their environments, whether that means organizing their spaces or tending to plants, encourages children to not just grow in self-discipline but also cultivate a respect for the "we" of living together. And this is all in accord with her basic premise that discipline cannot be imposed from on high and that it sprouts and grows only when the child himself thinks and acts in a way that he understands to be right and respectful.

The ideals of Montessori extend beyond the classroom and into family life, where countless golden chances exist for parents to rehearse her principles. When they do, they create a home setting where children learn the art of unambiguous, balanced, well-timed discipline. They create an environment where the children can learn in a secure, orderly space; in a space that is unfaltering—but not militant—in its guidance; in a space where trusted adults care about the children and where the children are encouraged to do what is obligatory and to make some of the choices that, in a just society, children should be free to make.

What this story shows is how discipline can be—an effective system of discipline that is not based on fear and compliance, that does not say, "Don't do that!," but rather, "Do this instead, and here are the reasons why." What it says to us is that if we want to have a discipline system in our schools that actually works, it has to be rooted in respect and understanding.

Implementing Consequences with Justice

Enforcing repercussions with justice necessitates a specialized style that tempers a call to account with a nod to compassion. In the parenting-by-the-book of the moment, this means ensuring that disciplinary actions are not only congruent with the misbehavior they are meant to address but also fair, understandable, and consistent with the way reasoned adults would expect a child to act, given the circumstances. Parenting experts advise us to work up to this ideal in an evaluative and reflective style, first considering the situation's context and "understanding our children's work habits and problem-solving styles."

Among the important principles that guide the establishment of just consequences is the one that demands proportional responses. When children go "off track," the adult response should be in direct relation to the severity and type of misbehavior. When, for instance, a child is in outright defiance concerning an important rule, that is a serious matter that calls for a serious response. This should not mean, however, that parents or caregivers fly off the handle or issue punishments that are, in effect, sending the child the message that there is no point in trying to behave because the consequences are so out of proportion to the seriousness of the child's behavior.

The way children perceive and internalize consequences often hinges on their emotional intelligence. When parents give out consequences, they should also have some discussions with their children about feelings and the impact of their actions—what's often referred to as "emotional coaching." This helps children become aware of their emotions and equips them with the tools to handle their emotions better. Parents who do this are effectively modeling emotional resilience. They're showing their children how to confront life challenges with grit instead of trying to hack or skirt around the obstacles. While this is good advice for all parents to follow, it's especially important and powerful for the parenting of children with an expressed or implied emotional disability.

Building a familial culture focused on core virtues necessitates stability and consistency in how fickle justice may be enacted within the home. When methods of discipline are delivered with fairness and clarity, it is more likely that the values parents wish to instill will actually take root. Equally important is having a set of shared family values that both defines a guiding framework for what shouldn't be done and a set of euphoric litmus tests for what should be done. And when these values are articulated, it is a good idea for parents and children to have a family summit just to make sure everyone is invested in the maintenance of a just family environment.

Finally, and importantly, virtuous conflict resolution is fundamental to carrying out discipline with justice. When conflicts arise, it's all too easy for parents to get flustered and to rush toward trying to settle things. Better to be prudent and to pursue open dialogue and serious, collaborative problem-solving among all the parties who need to have a say.

Yes, this does require patience, and it does require a good deal of discipline on the part of parents not to edge in with fixes. But the virtues of justice and fairness are reinforced when these practices are followed, because, indeed, the resolution of immediate threatening situations (such as the one that ignited a conflict in the first place) is one thing but establishing a culture in the family that respects law and order and also good old-fashioned discipline is another.

Three

Emotional Intelligence in Children

"Emotional intelligence is the ability to use emotions to enhance your thinking." John D. Mayer

Emotional intelligence, as articulated by John D. Mayer, is a profound capability that allows individuals to harness their emotions to sharpen their reasoning and decision-making. This concept resonates deeply with Stoic principles, which advocate for the mastery of one's emotions as a pathway to wisdom and virtue.

In the realm of childhood development, nurturing emotional intelligence becomes a vital task. Children, like unrefined materials, possess raw emotional responses that, when cultivated properly, can lead to enhanced self-awareness and resilience. The Stoics believed that emotions, if left unchecked, could cloud judgment and lead one astray. Therefore, teaching children to recognize and understand their emotional states aligns with the Stoic pursuit of clarity and rational thought.

By fostering emotional intelligence, we equip children to confront challenges with equanimity. Stoicism teaches us that external events are neutral; it is our perceptions that shape our emotional responses. When children learn to identify their emotions, they gain the power to respond thoughtfully rather than react impulsively. This self-regulation is essential for achieving personal goals and maintaining harmonious relationships.

Moreover, emotional intelligence cultivates empathy, a value highly esteemed in Stoicism. Understanding the emotions of others allows children to develop compassion and forge meaningful connections. The Stoic practice of viewing others as fellow travelers on the journey of life encourages a sense of shared humanity, which is foundational in the growth of healthy interpersonal dynamics.

In embracing emotional intelligence, children learn that their emotions are not mere whims to be indulged or suppressed. Instead, they become tools for introspection and growth. This aligns with the Stoic belief that true power lies in our ability to govern our inner lives. By integrating emotional intelligence into their lives, children can move toward becoming virtuous individuals, capable of making decisions that reflect wisdom rather than mere impulse.

Cultivating emotional intelligence in children, as highlighted by Mayer, is not simply an enhancement of cognitive ability but a foundational pillar supporting a life of virtue and reason. By instilling these principles, we prepare the next generation not only to navigate their own emotional landscapes but to contribute positively to the tapestry of human experience.

This statement captures the essence of emotional intelligence, underscoring its role in making better decisions and achieving more in life.

How emotional intelligence and Stoicism interact makes for a captivating dynamic. The tenets of Stoicism, with their emphasis on the supremacy of reason and the virtues of self-control, seem to offer a framework for understanding the relationship between the often irrational emotions that humans can experience and the calm and rational lives that Stoics encourage. Indeed, when one thinks about the not always obvious nature of the relationship between emotion and intelligence, the school of Stoic thought can be seen as a precursor to today's better-understood emotional and social intelligences.

From a psychological perspective, emotional intelligence encompasses the acknowledgment and comprehension of not just one's own feelings but also those of others—this aligns quite nicely with the Stoic tradition. Self-examination and mindfulness are age-old Stoic practices that, when harnessed, serve as the shared backbone for the kind of ascent to a higher state of being that both philosophies promise. Both the emotionally intelligent and the Stoics have access to that kind of civilization.

Furthermore, resilience is bolstered by both emotional intelligence and Stoicism. Emotional intelligence enables people to understand their emotions and situations and to adapt to them. Stoicism teaches acceptance of the unchangeable and control of the things that can be controlled. Together, these systems foster an understanding of life that is balanced, since emotions are acknowledged but don't drive decisions. And with that acknowledgment comes a deeper understanding of ourselves and our relationships with others. Consequently, enhanced relationships, better decisions, and a more fulfilling life are the likely outcomes of this emotional intelligence-Stoic combination.

The Importance of Emotional Intelligence

The ability to recognize, understand, and manage our emotions and the emotions of others is emotional intelligence (EI). In the family dynamic, EI is very essential for children to thrive because it allows for an understanding of core values like empathy, respect, and cooperation—values that are the bedrock of strong family relationships. Parents can prioritize EI and use it to their advantage in guiding their children through the rocky roads of their feelings and the equally rocky roads of other people's feelings.

Self-awareness is a key part of emotional intelligence. When parents are self-aware, they can identify and express their emotions. When parents model this practice, they encourage their children to do the same. Parents and children sitting together in a kitchen can put a private safe in those walls when it comes to open communication. If the family can openly talk about their different thoughts and emotions at any given moment, then that kitchen is a private safe. Kitchen conversations are only for those who live within the walls of that house. If you speak in the kitchen to someone else, you are breaking confidences. And with that example, I just broke an enormous taboo.

Understanding and sharing the feelings of others is another vital element of emotional intelligence. This is most commonly called empathy, and it is a component of emotional intelligence that one can certainly encourage in children. A good book to read with children is The Empathy Exams by Leslie Jamison. That is not true, and it is not a good book because it is good for children to read. It is a good book because it is good. It contains good writing, good plotting, and good characters. Yet what makes Leslie Jamison's book so important, so essential, is that everything it exhibits and that makes it a good book also exemplifies and expresses what empathy is. Which makes it a good book to read with children because what is empathy, and why is it important?

Bouncing back from setbacks and adapting to change are crucial aspects of resilience—Emotional intelligence is closely related to the resilience factor. Teaching children to manage their feelings in tough situations is an important way to help them develop the fortitude to overcome obstacles. Reflecting with children on their experiences and the emotions connected to those experiences—both good and bad—helps the child make sense of what happened at a brain level. This is a crucial part of resilience. It is like putting together a puzzle with a child; you are helping the child see the picture that will no doubt serve as a road map when he or she encounters a similar experience in the future.

At last, a familial atmosphere that centers on emotional intelligence enriches the home with an atmosphere of healthy oxygen, that is, the overall values and virtues of a family. Parents who encourage emotional understanding and skillful regulation of feelings promote first-rate emotional virtues. They raise children who are not only beasts of primarily interpersonal interactions but also harmful to no one. As these children grow, they develop emotional force fields that make them hard to approach (in a good way), which is what I mean by "tough." And as they grow older, those core values, along with the virtues of which I write in my book, serve them and all around them very well, making healthy homes and, I daresay, pleasant and interesting places to inhabit.

Encouraging Emotional Awareness

Promoting emotional awareness in kids is a core building block of their emotional intelligence and resilience. Yet right alongside it, we work to fortify their understanding of empathy—what it feels like when another person expresses a different emotion from yours, and what it means to them, and how it's not always easy to understand, but it is something we must practice and value. Our goal is to create a baseline where emotional awareness is the norm—a family virtue. My kids know that their dad has every right to be angry, hopeful, or sad, just as much as they do; that is on par with emotional intelligence.

To foster emotional awareness, parents can start by expressing their own emotions. Children learn by watching their parents, so when moms and dads say what they are feeling and handle the ups and downs of life with grace and style, they show their children the path toward emotional fluency. And when discussing emotions—whether they're feeling joy, frustration, or sadness—parents can encourage their children to feel that exploration is normal and worthwhile. This kind of talk promotes a culture of emotional literacy, allowing children to identify more readily and articulate better the kinds of emotions that are essential for their interpersonal relationships and overall well-being.

Besides being a source of behavioral modeling, parents can provide practice in emotional awareness through shared family activities. The family meal or game night can be a time for discussions about feelings that take on new meaning when parents have led with good, open-ended questions. Asked with genuine curiosity and interest, such questions can get children going on all kinds of conversations in which they might not otherwise engage. Family life—at least in those moments when it isn't busy with the mundane—is an opportunity for practice in emotional awareness. Take full advantage of it.

One more tried-and-true strategy for nurturing emotional awareness in kids is to set up a daily emotional check-in. Parents can set aside a few minutes each day for family members to share their emotions. They can converse about anything from how their day went to how they're feeling in general. Kids learn to articulate emotions during these conversations. The parents are modeling the practice of checking in with oneself and inquiring about the emotional well-being of others. Families are creating the stronghold of an emotional safe space.

Lastly, promoting emotional awareness means teaching kids about resilience in the context of their emotions. Children will invariably encounter obstacles and disappointments that elicit potent feelings. Parents can and should help them pinpoint these emotions—anger, sadness, fear, or whatever else might be coming up—when talking it through with the child. Better yet, guide the child in having a conversation with themselves about their emotions. Not only does this make it more likely that they'll actually understand and remember the process next time, but it also instills the values of thoughtful problem-solving and healthy emotional expression in these young children.

The Goleman Effect

Within the domain of human existence, the interplay of intellect and emotion seems to direct our journey. But what, then, is the contribution of Daniel Goleman? Goleman is a psychologist who also understands the craft of science journalism. He has done far more than many of us could hope to do in casting light on the very darkened corners of the idea of something called Emotional Intelligence, or EI, for short. Probably, most of you have heard of EI. Some of you may have even read or skimmed Goleman's best-selling book, "Emotional Intelligence: Why It Can Matter More Than IQ."

The philosophical journey that Goleman undertook to understand the nature of emotional intelligence began with his own experiences as a journalist. The pursuit of knowledge took him from the domain of neuroscience to the field of psychology, where he became enthralled by the powerful dance of emotional processes. The brain's responses to emotional stimuli not only dictate our thoughts and actions at the moment but also have long-lasting effects. Of this, he is certain. And while the ancient Greeks and Romans mustered powerful insights about the nature of emotions like love, anger, and hatred, our understanding of the brain's structure and function has revealed just how deeply entrenched human emotions are in that ancient seat of emotion, the amygdala.

What delineates Goleman from the large field of emotional intelligence is his investigation into its cultivation, particularly during the vulnerable developmental years of childhood. He argues that emotional intelligence has at its core several foundational components:

1. Being aware: Knowing what kind of emotional state you're in.

2. Being not quite as aware, or maybe even in denial, about how much you might be tempering your emotions: This is the male mode of self-regulation.

3. Not being in touch with the male way of navigating self-regulation can stop a woman from seeing the connection between her emotional state and the states of the men around her, which wreaks havoc on empathy.

Goleman asserts that these elements are not innate gifts conferred on a select few but rather skills that anyone can nurture and develop with intention and practice. A premise that dates back as early as the Stoic's, with the axiom that virtue is a skill, not a simple trait of character.

The insights of Goleman reach well past the individual and light the way to some collective flourishing. He is crystal clear in making the case that emotional intelligence is not just good for the 'you' side of the 'me and you' equation but is also half of the 'you' that we really need to value for academic achievement. Goleman cites numerous researchers, for whom EI is the real deal, to argue as forcefully as he can that it is indeed a vital part of pathways leading to everyone's flourishing. He makes a very good point—rather, he makes several very good points—that we should not just ignore feelings in our classrooms but rather embrace the extremely important role that emotional intelligence plays in helping children achieve personal and academic success.

Goleman's work provides an exceptional framework for giving children the kind of EI that he, in many ways, shows is integral for success. He is not against the kind of dressing-up-Ivy-logic that gets people into Harvard, Yale, and Princeton. He is profoundly in favor of supporting a holistic kind of smarts that combines the cognitive and the EI realms of intelligence. Goleman's work underscores the importance of our offspring not only becoming smart, as in getting good grades, but also becoming good at life—life as in "how to get through it" without going nuts or doing other people harm, which, when you think about it, is one profound way of becoming a decent person.

Daniel's narrative reveals the deep meaning of emotional intelligence in the young mind's development. Goleman's work gives not just a theoretical foundation but also practical guidance to those who would help serve the next generation. He places an emphasis on not just awareness of emotions but also on the kind of regulation that leads to the cultivation of better relationships and an enhanced sense of personal success. Advocacy for emotional intelligence is not new, but Goleman's is one of the most well-known.

Teaching Empathy and Compassion

It is vitally important to teach empathy and compassion if we want to foster emotional intelligence and resilience in children. These core virtues not only enhance interpersonal relationships but also contribute to a family's overall harmony. Empathy allows children to understand and share the feelings of others. Compassion motivates them to act and alleviate suffering. It's not too much to say that these two qualities are the absolute bedrock of social navigation and the formation of connections with other human beings.

The parents can model empathetic behavior in their daily interactions to teach empathy effectively. Demonstrating active listening and validating feelings and discussing different kinds of perspectives during family conversations can have a profound impact on a child's developing ability to empathize. Moreover, kids can partake in community service or volunteer work. These direct observational experiences about someone else's struggles can also have an enormous impact on a child's developing sense of empathy. Seeing firsthand and understanding someone else's struggles allow the kinds of diverse life situations that reinforce the underestimated importance of empathy in our society.

Compassion can also be cultivated through organized family activities that encourage kindness and generosity. Parents can set the stage for these sorts of family projects, using local charitable organizations and other means to help not just family members, but also people in the community and beyond. I think our family has enough going on that we don't really need to do these sorts of projects; in fact, my parents probably do these sorts of things as part of their jobs. But considering that is forcing us to do this, I think we have some grounds for complaint.

Moreover, it is vital to instruct children on how to identify and communicate their emotions if one aims to develop empathy and compassion in children. Parents can help their children achieve emotional intelligence through the use of emotion charts (which display various feelings), storytelling (in which children and parents act out scenarios), and even role-playing (where children mimic their parents and vice versa in front of a mirror). After these practices, when the safe parent-child environment has been established, emotional literacy should be ascertained through open dialogue.

In the end, nurturing "empathy and compassion" proves consistent with the "principles of [virtue] parenting." The authors of this guidebook for prospective and practicing parents set great store by these two values, which they consider "essential for any emotionally intelligent child." Moreover, they see variables like gratitude, resilience, and emotional intelligence as intimately intertwined. As they put it, "If you are resilient, you bounce back from setbacks; if you are emotionally intelligent, you know when to ask for help in bouncing back; and if you are compassionate, you help yourself and the people around you get back on their feet."

Four

Building Resilience

"The purpose of life is not happiness; it is usefulness." Jordan Peterson

Jordan Peterson has stated, "The purpose of life is not happiness; it is usefulness." This perspective underscores the notion that life's true resilience isn't found in a relentless pursuit of ephemeral pleasures but instead in a meaningful engagement with life and a contribution to a cause or purpose that has implications far beyond one's immediate personal space. This focus on living a life of usefulness—a life directed toward the service of something larger than oneself—seems to be a good recipe for the cultivation of a too-often-absent sense of fulfillment.

Peterson's view aligns with a number of psychological principles. One important principle is the notion that adversity and suffering are fundamental to the human experience. Accepting and confronting difficulties rather than shunning them can lead not just to coping as one might do under "easy conditions," but to genuine and hard-won growth, a kind of growth that one might also find in the concept of post-traumatic growth.

At a basic level, Peterson is a psychologist. He has spent a good part of his life helping people overcome personal problems. And though he draws on many philosophical and religious texts, he typically returns to the exhortation that his clients should clean up their domestic kingdoms and set their lives in order.

This injunction is not just good advice: it is existentially meaningful. It is a way for individuals to realize their latent potential and to take on the mantle of responsibility that he thinks every person ought to bear.

From the perspective of psychology, resilience is not just a trait but also a skill that can be developed. We see diverse life paths in people with resilience—yet what they share is practice in a series of essential psychological and interpersonal behaviors (or a path to learning those behaviors through trial and error). Copiously demonstrating these skills in otherwise ordinary conditions lays the appearance of resilience over their lives. The "strong network of relationships" these people maintain; the "easy, positive outlook" they tend to have; the path they have walked to a suite of effective, if not always easy, psychological coping strategies. These are the core ingredients of an appearance of resilience.

The way personal responsibility, the quest for significance, and the acceptance of suffering interact with each other showcases the complex nature of resilience. This is something Peterson has been saying for a while, and it has taken on new significance in his recent book. He articulates it as a certain interplay among three elements:

Understanding Resilience

The quality of resilience is critical because it makes children able to deal with the problems and setbacks of life. To understand resilience, one must perceive it not merely as the ability to come back from hard times but as a combination of skills and qualities that make for a return-to-function state. These skills include emotional regulation, the ability to problem-solve, and a consistently positive outlook. Resilience can be "parented." This means that virtuous parents can make resilience a characteristic of their child. Importantly, modern psychologists have a good handle on which parental virtues help make a child resilient. These are the same parental virtues that are good for helping all children, not just those who might face hard times, because those virtues help children face life on its own terms.

One of the most important elements of building resilience is emotional intelligence. Parents can help their children build this crucial skill by teaching them to identify and express emotions. When children understand the full range of feelings, the environment they live in is understandable and comprehensible. It is normal to feel sad or disappointed following a setback. But when parents create a space for their children to discuss feelings, those children develop not only an understanding of their emotions but also empathy for others. It is easy to be overwhelmed by anger or sadness, but when children learn to cope with those feelings, they are building resilience.

Another essential approach to developing resilience is fostering a growth mindset. When children learn to see challenges as chances to grow rather than as impossible problems, they are much more likely to push through the hard times. Telling kids to love their mistakes and to use them as stepping stones—this was the way they did it when I was a kid, and I think it's still a valid approach—reinforces the idea that effort pays off. The persistence that leads us to try, try again (in the face of setbacks) is the kind of determination I think we all want our children to possess.

Additionally, creating a family culture focused on fundamental virtues fosters a propitious environment for resilience to take root and flourish. Families that value kinds of things like justice, temperance, and prudence help their children understand the importance of such virtues not only as a family members for whom these kinds of decisions and behaviors are a matter of course but also as future citizens in a diverse society. With this understanding, conflict and other significant challenges the children face become opportunities to experiment with these virtues. They may not always succeed, but failure with these kinds of challenges provides a safe space for learning.

Teaching gratitude is very important when it comes to building resilience. When children learn to recognize not just what they want, but also what they have, and when they learn that it is just as important to acknowledge the positive aspects of their lives as it is to express what they wish were different, they are better able to negotiate the ups and downs of life. What could be more valuable in the life of a child than a mindset that recognizes the worth of life itself? A child's acknowledgment of gratitude also contributes to the child's understanding of the "gift of life," which is one of the greatest gifts any child can receive from a parent.

A Pattern for Success

General George S. Patton is an icon of American history, personifying the kind of unbending spine and grit that Stoics equate with true strength. When most people would have crumpled under the pressures and dire circumstances of World War II—faced with a slew of nearly insurmountable military challenges that many quite understandably would have interpreted as signs of impending defeat and failure—Patton held fast. He did not yield; he did not brake in the face of what would have been a very human and understandable meltdown. And for that, he is admired as one of our great wartime leaders.

Patton's illustrious career reached a peak during the Battle of the Bulge in December 1944, when the German Army unexpectedly counteroffensive in the Ardennes. The Allied forces found themselves in great trouble. But Patton, commanding his Third Army from the south, did not falter. Instead, he embodied the Stoic ideal of taking action in the face of chaos. Even though it was winter, even though supplies were low, even though the assault was unexpected, the 3rd Army pushed forward, in just three days, over 100 miles, to relieve the town of Bastogne. This was not just a remarkable military achievement. It was also a manifestation of Patton's indomitable spirit and his commitment to his men.

Patton's resilience was a two-edged sword. On one side was physical endurance; on the other was psychological fortitude. He practiced and preached the power of positive thinking. This notion is deeply rooted in Stoic philosophy. Stoicism emphasizes the importance of maintaining a virtuous mind under the most difficult external conditions. Patton's personal writing clearly reveals his conviction that "the only thing we have to fear is fear itself." This is, of course, not a new idea. It is an old idea that has been passed down from generation to generation. In essence, it says that when it comes to courage, the mind is the master.

Setbacks did not dampen Patton's resolve. He met the most notorious of these, when he was forced to apologize for having berated a soldier afflicted with battle fatigue, and emerged undeterred from that low point. Indeed, Patton did not really believe in low points. For him, they are not anything more than moments that suck and then, hopefully, are succeeded by better moments. His main belief was that the bounce-back has to be higher than the initial fall. And if my Stoic memory serves me correctly, that is more or less how he stated it. The essence of the Patton bounce-back was that it had to be a clearly defined "success."

The narrative that Patton gives is a captivating picture of resilience. He is someone who refused to allow setbacks—whether personal or professional—to dictate his trajectory. Each obstacle in his path, it seems, became a crucible for growth, an opportunity for him to demonstrate how well he could lead under duress and how effectively he could get his men to press on when the odds were against them. My impression is that Patton never knew the meaning of the phrase "giving up," and that his influence on those with whom he served was to instill in them a similar mindset of positivity and tenacity.

For anyone in a position of guidance—parents, for instance—Patton's legacy offers an abundance of leading-the-way moments to remember. Above all, they might reflect on the virtues of leadership, resilience, and confronting adversity head-on. His motivating of troops during the darkest hours of the conflict shows that resilience isn't just about physical endurance; it's the mental gumption to keep going when, in Bickel's words, "the odds seem stacked against you." Both Bickel and parents willing to take this lesson to heart insist embracing it starts with rearing children in a way that instills the same virtues in them.

Patton's life was filled with both controversy and crisis, yet it stands as a clear testament to resilience and perseverance. He was the kind of leader that most people could only dream of being. He led not always by way of example (many wouldn't want their children to emulate Patton), but he led in the way that a legion of soldiers could respect. And he respected them back.

Consider Patton's journey. You know, Patton is a great symbol of American resilience. Why? Because it's not that he never had adversity. Patton had plenty of it. Patton had adversity and yet still managed to be...to rise and learn and to go ahead with the commands that he had. And most reasons that we might look for are reasons such as: he had good training at West Point. He had a favorable family background. He had an intelligent wife. He had plenty of money. He had an easy life. All of these things are not really true. They're not really true because: Resilience is really all about what happens in the brain.

Strategies for Fostering Fortitude

Building strength in children is crucial for their growth into resilient and able adults. One effective way to do this is to foster an environment that encourages facing life's many challenges head-on. This means not always rushing in to solve problems for children and letting kids feel and experience what it's like to work through tough situations. When children take on and work through challenging experiences, they build up the mental and emotional muscles necessary for handling the next life obstacle that comes their way. These experiences give children the opportunity to learn from mistakes and, when it comes to tough situations, gift children the growth and grit that will serve them well in the future.

Another vital strategy is to model resilience. Children learn a lot from watching their parents and caregivers. When adults are very visible in carrying out the business of resilience—coping with work stress, say, or muddling through a demanding life transition—they provide the kids in their lives with a compelling example of how to get through tough times. Imagine the family dinner table during a typical work week. Parents and kids alike are tired and trying to eat and discuss the day's ups and downs. The table is an excellent platform for a work-stress-panic-but-keep-moving-through-resilience civics lesson, complete with sound effects.

It is very important to promote problem-solving skills when we are trying to foster fortitude. When children face conflicts or challenges, it is tempting for parents to step in and resolve the matter. Instead, parents can work with the children to push through the problem and arrive at a satisfactory solution. This simple act can foster critical thinking and resilience because it forces the children to evaluate some pretty important options and consequences. These same acts of 'solving' work just as well when the act is done in tandem with a school-age child as when the parent does them solo with the preschooler on her lap. As with reading, though, the acts of 'doing' an imaginary problem and 'doing' it correctly (or not) make us critical thinkers and problem solvers.

Another key strategy for fostering grit is creating a community where children feel safe and secure. Young people need to connect with other people their age and interact with a diverse range of individuals. To that end, parents should encourage their children to engage with their peers, both in one-on-one situations and in group settings. The more a child interacts with the world at large, the more opportunities there are to practice key components of grit, like persistence, overcoming obstacles, and bouncing back from failure, in a context where it's safe to take risks and make mistakes.

Lastly, nurturing gratitude can significantly boost a child's ability to confront obstacles. By consistently directing their children's attention toward what they should be thankful for, parents can help them develop a mindset that is positively resilient toward adversity. This practice not only fosters emotional intelligence but also underpins the idea that even tough times can yield truly valuable lessons. By making gratitude a normal part of their family's life, parents can carry their children through to the other side of some challenges just by putting their life's focus back on its more "positive" side.

Encouraging a Growth Mindset

Promoting a growth mindset within the family helps foster resilience and emotional intelligence and creates a culture of continuous learning. A growth mindset, as defined by psychologist Carol Dweck, is the belief that abilities and intelligence can be developed through dedication and hard work. This mindset not only helps cultivate a love for learning but also promotes perseverance and adaptability—core nurturing virtues of the parenting of my generation. Parents today can instill a growth mindset in their children by embracing challenges and viewing failures as opportunities for growth, and by and large, modeling these attitudes themselves.

Balanced discipline that embodies understanding and fairness is a key to promoting a growth mindset at home. Parents who are solely consequence-driven don't cultivate an environment in which children feel safe to risk failure. And if children don't feel safe to fail, they can't truly grow. Kids have to be allowed to make mistakes. But when using balanced discipline, parents also have to engage their children in discussions about those mistakes. Framing the post-error dialogue as "a conversation about learning vs. a conversation about performance" tips the balance toward resilience. And framing has a huge impact on the growth mindset.

One important facet of promoting a growth mindset is the kind of language parents use to praise their children. When parents commend their children, they do well to avoid congratulating them for simply being very good at something, as in saying, "You are so good at that." Instead, when they talk to their children about being proud of them, they focus on the kind of growth they want to see and the conditions that make it more likely to occur. "I am proud of how hard you worked," or "You really persevered through that challenge," are the sorts of things they might say.

The development of a "growth mindset" is supported by a family culture built on "core virtues and shared values." Parents can help cultivate a growth mindset in their children by engaging them in discussions about "the importance of virtues such as temperance, fortitude, and justice." More and more writers are using the term "virtuous" to describe parenting that molds children into better people. It has the added benefit of not naming one particular religion or another since, as far as I know, no religion has claimed a monopoly on the "core virtues" mentioned most often in this literature: temperance, fortitude, and justice.

In sum, nurturing gratitude within the family is essential to instilling a growth mindset. When children are not just told but also shown that it is good to savor the moments we just lived, they in turn (1) learn the value of embracing the present and (2) better appreciate the delightful, routine, and even challenging moments that comprise their family life. At the heart of these gratitude practices is an emphasis on recognizing the value of our past experiences—both the positive ones and those that at the moment seemed negative. And alas, navigating family life without a little of each is impossible!

Five

Family Values and Virtues

"Family is not an important thing, it's everything."
Michael J Fox.

Family, as the foundation of our existence, embodies the stoic principles of virtue. In recognizing that "Family is not an important thing, it's everything," we acknowledge that our relationships are not mere connections but essential elements that shape our character and guide our actions. Stoicism teaches us that virtue is the highest good, and it is within the family unit that we often first encounter the practice of virtue.

The family is a crucible for the development of essential virtues such as wisdom, courage, justice, and temperance. Through our interactions with family members, we learn to navigate the complexities of human emotions and the responsibilities that come with love and care. The challenges faced within familial relationships provide opportunities to cultivate patience and understanding, essential traits for a virtuous life.

In the context of stoicism, virtue is not only about personal integrity but also about our duty to others. Acknowledging the central role of family compels us to act with virtue towards our loved ones.

FAMILY VALUES AND VIRTUES

We are reminded to exercise kindness and compassion, to support one another in times of difficulty, and to celebrate each other's successes. These actions contribute to the greater good, not only for our families but also for the community at large.

Moreover, the notion of family extends beyond biological ties. Stoicism encourages us to find a sense of kinship with all humanity, recognizing that the virtues we nurture within our families can be extended to our broader interactions. In this way, the principle that family is everything reinforces our responsibility to embody virtue in all our relationships.

In embracing the significance of family, we align ourselves with a stoic perspective that values the cultivation of character through our closest bonds. By prioritizing family and the virtues that arise from those relationships, we build a foundation for a meaningful life, grounded in the principles of stoicism. Thus, as we strive for personal excellence, we must remember that our families are not just important; they are the very essence of our journey toward virtue.

In the context of psychology, family serves as the primary social unit where individuals first learn about trust, love, and responsibility. Positive family interactions foster emotional well-being and resilience, while dysfunctional dynamics can lead to psychological issues. The support and understanding found within a family can significantly influence one's self-esteem and coping mechanisms.

From a stoic perspective, the family is seen as a microcosm of the larger world. Stoicism teaches the importance of virtue, self-control, and rationality, which can be applied to family dynamics. For instance, practicing patience and understanding within the family can help manage conflicts and promote harmony. Stoics emphasize the significance of duty towards one's family, viewing it as a way to develop moral character and contribute to the greater good.

The interplay between these psychological insights and stoic principles highlights the importance of nurturing family relationships. By cultivating virtues such as empathy, patience, and responsibility, individuals can create a supportive family environment that not only strengthens bonds but also fosters personal growth and resilience. This dual perspective encourages a holistic approach to family values, integrating emotional and rational aspects for a more profound understanding of familial relationships.

Identifying Core Family Values

In psychology, family is considered the fundamental social unit where individuals first experience trust, love, and responsibility. Learning these basic human values occurs in the context of positive family interactions. These interactions lay the foundation for emotional well-being and resilience, which are necessary for one to thrive in this psychologically challenging world. Conversely, when one learns these values in the context of family dysfunction, the ensuing psychological issues can sometimes ripple out to affect an entire community.

A stoic outlook on life sees the family as a smaller version of the world at large. Stoicism teaches that the way to be is virtuous, that self-control is a keystone of a good life, and that one must always hold fast to rationality, come what may. It is a combination of tremendous (if not always spectacular) moral resources that the Stoic cultivates in order to manage not only family but also world affairs. The Stoics especially highlight the necessity of patience and understanding. "How can a family function well," they ask, "if its members do not possess those two crucial qualities?"

The correlation of these psychological understandings and stoic principles underscores the value of family ties. When individuals associate with their family, they need to act with virtues such as empathy, patience, and responsibility. These seem to be the minimum requirements for a family relationship to be supportive. From another angle, these qualities also strengthen the basis of the nudges and shove as the family member becomes more likely to fulfill promises and be there during hard times. Whether nudging or shoving, the family member is acting with virtues that allow both him or her and the other family member to grow as persons in what has been described as a "resilient family."

A foundational step in nurturing a virtuous household is identifying core family values. These values are the guiding principles that shape behavior, decision-making, and the overall family dynamic. Families must start with open discussions about what virtues matter most to them—e.g. prudence, temperance, fortitude, and justice. Engaging in this conversation as a family ensures that every member has a stake in the process. And it also reinforces the two-way street that is fundamental to problem-solving with children: at the outset, parents express their values and virtues that the household is founded upon, and at the next stage, children learn to articulate the values that matter to them.

After families have pointed out potential core values, it is essential to look at them through the lens of practical application. Consider how these values show up in everyday life and in family interactions. For instance, if justice is a core value, families should take a long, hard look at how they handle conflicts and disagreements. Are decisions made fairly and equitably? Do parents model justice in their discipline of the children, providing them with a clear understanding of the consequences of their actions? These are but a few of the many questions families might reflect upon as they work to ensure that the stated core values are indeed lived out.

These core values can be made more solid by incorporating them into familial routines. A key means of achieving that is through regular family meetings. At those gatherings, it can be helpful to discuss the core values and what they mean, as well as to celebrate them. Sharing even mundane experiences in which any family member exhibited a virtue like "gratitude" or "resilience" can be powerful, too—not unlike how the National Football League might momentarily honor players who are extraordinarily charitable as "Good Guys." Parents can also make use of everyday situations as teaching moments, guiding their children in applying the core values in real world contexts.

Recognizing the specific contributions of each family member is a vital part of nurturing family values. Encouraging children to take ownership of and be proud of their values is another important aspect. When children are young, it is very important for them to feel that they are leading the family as much as the parents are, when it comes to decisions about family values. It can be very empowering for a child to lead a family discussion about what virtues aren't just for the parents, but also for the children, and how these virtues can be practiced by them.

Pinpointing and cultivating fundamental family values is a never-ending process. The family unit may grow and change; it doesn't have to stay the same. Yet, even if a family model is remolded, the values that inspire familial affection should be preserved. Reflection and reassessment are essential to close any realignment that may have occurred between the family and its core values. Fortunately, creating a prudent, temperate, fortitudinous, and just family culture is nothing more than an ongoing exercise in open communication. In doing this, children learn resilient emotional intelligence—the kind that will carry them beyond the context of family life in the end.

The Rothchild Legacy

The Rothschild family is one of the few in human history to have been profoundly influential, and their legacy is not merely a matter of financial prowess but also a matter of virtuous, principled living. This illustrious lineage is helmed by Mayer Amschel Rothschild, whose endeavors in the late 18th century in Frankfurt, Germany, laid the foundation for a banking empire that has reverberated through time. Yet, the real distinction of the Rothschild family is not the accumulation of wealth but the maintenance of long-term integrity, trust, and a vision that goes beyond the ephemeral nature of material success.

Mayer Amschel Rothschild understood that real prosperity is based on virtue—not on the appearance of virtue or on words alone, but on the kind of virtue that is proved and tested in the everyday world where business is done. The assertion most commonly attributed to him regarding the primacy of financial control—"Give me control of a nation's money, and I care not who makes its laws"—is not, in fact, an expression of an unhinged ambition to dominate and rule. Rather, it encodes and expresses a recognition of the profound moral weight that comes with financial stewardship. With this, I think, we can hear a stoic ancestor of the modern Business School saying that financial responsibility is a serious business and that one doesn't pass the buck lightly if one wishes to retain the kind of integrity that makes the Rothschild name prosper for centuries.

The Rothschild family ethos extends beyond simple trade; it is an all-encompassing way of life that prizes not just the accumulation of wealth but also the quest for knowledge and the cultivation of character. Mayer Amschel Rothschild understood the true transformative power of education. He ensured that his children learned not just business savvy but also the arts of critical and creative thinking, the virtue of moral facileness, and a kind of public citizenship that endowed them with the authority to serve their communities. Every generation since Rothschild has preserved his model of intellectual growth and ethical development.

What distinguishes the Rothschild legacy is not just the wealth that it has amassed, but the far-seeing wisdom with which it has governed that wealth, a wisdom that has allowed the family to maintain not just an impressive capital base over many generations but also a splendid public image. By "public image," I do not mean that the Rothschilds are better at spin than the rest of us; I mean that they have maintained this public image and that if they had hired the firm of Robinson, Wood, Aiken, and Moore to do a Rothschild public relations job, this firm would not have needed to work very hard.

Equally important was their deep sense of family responsibility. In the midst of their financial empire, they cultivated a familial bond, ensuring that each generation had not just access to material resources but also to the wisdom and support of their kin. This approach to shared success made them resilient against the political and economic tempests that have buffeted so many other dynasties. It enabled the family to stay together in an age of individualism and to pursue, with a remarkable unity of purpose, a set of ideals that we will also pursue in this chapter.

The story of the Rothschilds serves as a powerful reminder of how family values can shape an enduring legacy. The Rothschilds went beyond the construction of a mere financial empire (one that, by the way, holds many secrets of the astonishing type that would make the creators of pre-World War II Marvel Comics green with envy). The Rothschilds constructed a culture of virtue that has influenced, for the better, a multitude of lives—only God knows how many lives. The Rothschilds culled together virtues such as integrity, trust, education, and foresight. They were not short on those virtues.

Today's parents can look to the Rothschild family's story for a powerful example of how to instill a culture of virtue in their homes. The Rothschilds, a banking family whose fortune dates back to the 18th century, have a long history of not just multiplying their riches but also of maintaining and passing down through the generations a remarkable set of principles. Although the family is not without blemish—several of its members were staunch supporters of the British Empire and the Nazis in World War I and II, respectively—it is more noteworthy for having produced a long line of individuals who have done a great deal of good (and, in many instances, not called a lot of attention to themselves in doing so).

Creating a Family Culture of Virtue

A family culture of virtue starts with the establishment of a shared understanding of core values. Among the secret ingredients that make family life successful, I would list this one near the top: the secret of shared family core values. With this understanding as the foundation, you can then build a family culture of virtue where character development is the norm. Otherwise virtuous families may just drift in the direction of least resistance and end up settling for superficial conversations about right and wrong. Building a family core of values takes time. You can get the process started with these three steps: 1. Talk About It. 2. Make Time for It. 3. Mind the Language.

In a culture of virtue, misbehavior can't simply be dealt with as it comes up; it's necessary to reinforce what the culture stands for. There are several techniques that parents can use to accomplish this:

1. **Set Clear Expectations**: Let your children know what kinds of behavior are acceptable and what kinds aren't. Say what you mean and mean what you say.

2. **Use Consistent Consequences**: When they step over the line, give them a time-out and let them "unwind." Don't let the misbehavior stand or go unchallenged.

3. **Reflection Opportunities**: Ask them questions that lead them to understand that the culture of virtues isn't just some kind of arbitrary imposition.

When parents do these things, they're modeling the kinds of virtues that lead children to remember what's right when nobody's looking.

Another key component of establishing a family culture of virtue is emotional intelligence. Every family needs to cultivate an environment that fosters the children's abilities to recognize and manage emotions. After all, the amount of resilience and empathy exhibited by the children will find root in their emotional intelligence. Parents can heavily influence the development of their children's EI through discussion. And EI can find its way into any family's culture when it is part of the core conversation. "What do you think about that, emotionally? How does that make you feel? How do you think the other person feels? What do you think about expressing your feelings in that way?"

Cultivating resilience in children is crucial for their development and incipient ability to manage life's many challenges. Parents can promote resilience by nurturing a growth mindset, where value is placed on effort and perseverance rather than immediate success. When children face setbacks, parents should assist them in reflecting on their experiences, identifying the lessons learned, and setting new, go-for-it goals. This process not only fortifies their resilience but also enshrines the virtues of prudence and temperance as they learn to manage many types of adversity. And if not managed with maximum gusto, a family culture that celebrates effort and resilience is an atmosphere where children feel empowered to confront any myriad of obstacles.

Ultimately, nurturing a sense of gratitude in the household is an incredibly effective way to bring about the virtues of prudence and temperance. When children are encouraged to express their appreciation for the vast array of experiences, relationships, and opportunities that life brings, it seems to kind of hardwire them into recognizing the good that exists in reality. Although our family does something on a daily basis that is even more elevated in terms of promoting an appreciation for the things we have, I still find this practice mentioned in the book to be very good. I really like the idea of keeping a journal and expressing something about why we are grateful to God for that at the end of the day.

The Role of Rituals in Reinforcing Values

The family structure receives powerful reinforcement from core values that hold it together. Values are instilled through rituals, which are nothing more than the repeated performance of an act that carries meaning. The act becomes a shorthand expression of what the family believes and the principles it stands for. Instructions like "be a good sport" or "keep your promises" are pretty elongated expressions of what the family stands for. And they serve what I call the "four-way test" for every act, which ultimately defines the family: Is it fair? Is it kind? Is it something I would want to do if I were in the other person's shoes? Family rituals are a significant means of promoting emotional intelligence in children.

One hardly could find a more potent way to "cultivate good soil," as one father of a family practicing rituals put it. The regular family dinner, for example, is a stage upon which the open communication that Carolyn McCauley finds so vital can take place. Children can express their thoughts and feelings. And just listen: Can you imagine a world in which every child has the experience of their parents publicly valuing whatever form of "stupid" (as one psychologist puts it) that child's expression of thought or feeling might take?

It can be beneficial to include rituals that stress resilience. Remembering to celebrate accomplishments, both significant and minor, is a good way to remind ourselves and our children that we are capable of achieving what we set out to do. This sort of tradition reaffirms the value of courage, determination, and problem-solving in the face of what appear to be insurmountable obstacles. Going beyond the personal realm, what would it mean to articulate a national tradition of resilience? What significant moments would we include at the head of the line?

In addition, efficient tools can be used to teach balanced discipline. Consistent disciplinary practices signal justice and temperance. One-of-a-kind family meetings can discuss rules and consequences. Such meetings can be a cover for discipline disguised as family togetherness. Under this cover, children can be encouraged to understand the rationale behind boundaries. The child can be prompted to make a series of "decisions" that signal the family saying "no" to some of the decisions the child could make at some times in some contexts. The decisions the family signals with such meetings can be done with fairness and gentility.

Lastly, shared rituals can boost gratitude and cement a family's commitment to living virtuously. When families regularly express gratitude, the simple act of recognizing the gifts of life has a way of nudging individuals toward the generous and kind behavior that is the content of temperance. That is to say, gratitude gives a family member the right disposition for being nice. One could go way overboard and say that gratitude is the secret sauce for achieving family nirvana. But it is not, and we must not oversell it.

Six

Virtuous Conflict Resolution

"Conflict is the start of awareness." - Mary Caroline Richards

Conflict serves as a crucible for self-examination and growth, revealing the underlying truths of our character. In the face of discord, we are compelled to confront our beliefs, values, and the emotional reactions that arise. This confrontation, while often uncomfortable, is essential for the cultivation of virtue, a central tenet of Stoic philosophy.

The Stoics teach that virtue is the highest good and consists of wisdom, courage, justice, and temperance. In moments of conflict, the opportunity to practice these virtues becomes apparent. Wisdom guides us to see beyond the immediate turmoil, allowing us to discern the causes of the conflict and the perspectives of others. It encourages a rational approach to resolution, where we seek understanding rather than victory.

Courage is necessitated in conflict as it requires us to face uncomfortable truths about ourselves and others. It takes strength to engage in difficult conversations, to admit faults, and to embrace

VIRTUOUS CONFLICT RESOLUTION

vulnerability. This courage fosters resilience, enabling us to navigate the turbulence of disagreement with equanimity.

Justice, a cornerstone of Stoic virtue, calls us to act fairly in conflict. It urges us to consider the needs and rights of all involved, striving for a resolution that honors the dignity of each person. In doing so, we transcend our egos and foster a sense of community, recognizing that our interconnectedness is a source of strength.

Temperance plays a vital role in conflict resolution as well. It tempers our impulses and emotional responses, allowing us to respond thoughtfully rather than react impulsively. By practicing moderation in our emotions and actions, we maintain clarity and composure, which are essential for productive dialogue.

Thus, conflict, rather than being merely an obstacle, emerges as a profound teacher. It illuminates our path toward personal development and moral integrity. By embracing conflict with a Stoic mindset, we transform potential discord into an opportunity for virtuous engagement, ultimately deepening our understanding of ourselves and our relationships with others. In this way, conflict indeed becomes the start of awareness, leading us toward the practice of virtue in all aspects of life.

Disagreement among family members can be a positive force. It can lead to growth and increased awareness. Disagreements among groups of people—like families—can have virtuous outcomes if the groups involved work through the disagreements and arrive at resolutions. The family dynamic can be jump-started into growth mode by the presence of a disagreement that is followed by a period of conflict resolution.

Psychologically, the family often serves as the principal environment for personal development. When handled with a listening and understanding disposition, conflict can foster emotional intelligence and resilience. Conflict encourages family members to express themselves and can help the family system create a culture of open and honest communication. Some families develop a "no secrets" policy, which is a way of signaling that all members can count on one another to communicate openly and without fear.

This approach to conflict resolution can be enriched by stoic philosophy, especially its ideas about acceptance and rationality. Stoicism teaches that one should concentrate on what is truly within one's control and that one should meet life's challenges with not just any composure but the kind of unflappable calm that can come only through rational thinking. In a family, applying these principles means recognizing that conflicts are bound to occur but that they can be handled in a mindset of cool-headedness. Instead of meeting a slight with an emotionally satisfying comeback, a family member might counter with clarity and reason, seeing the slight as something that might just be an opportunity for personal and familial growth.

These potent psychological aspects, when combined with the stoic family principles upon which I base my work, highlight what I believe to be a remarkably healthy dynamic in our family. Conflicts are not just tolerated; they are encouraged, within reason, to serve as a kind of familial rite of passage. "No family is going to get along all the time," I tell the kids. "If we did, we wouldn't be a family; we'd be a cult. And if we don't argue, what's the point of having strong and weak personalities, or any personalities, for that matter?"

Strategies for Effective Communication

A stone corner of virtuous parenting is effective communication. It allows the transmission of values and makes strong family ties possible. To communicate well, parents must listen well—actively. This means more than just hearing the words that children say. It means understanding their good sense and also their not-so-good sense. But, better yet, it means understanding the unfathomable depths that children usually achieve when communicating with the parent whose ear is really listening. To gain these depths, the parents should engage in conversations with the children that are better described as "emotional intelligence drills."

Yet another key tactic involves using language that is clear and appropriate for the child's age. Communicating with a child at the level of their developmental stage not only helps them understand but also gives them the impression that the talk was tailored just for them, which builds trust and makes the child more receptive to what is being said. When parents tell children what the expectations are, what the boundaries are, and what the values are in a way that makes these things resonate, then the child incorporates all of this into their understanding of the parental unit as a secure entity that provides reliable guidance.

Effective family interactions hinge on more than just verbal communication; they also necessitate competence in the alternative mode of expression: non-verbal communication. This mode of expression comprises body language, facial expressions, and tone—elements that arguably covey emotions and attitudes far more powerfully than words alone. Parents, in particular, need to be mindful of their non-verbal cues, for these either enhance or undermine the messages they wish to impart. For instance, warmth and openness can be expressed far more powerfully by non-verbal means than by words. Yet it is possible to coordinate non-verbal cues and verbal messages to create around family communication the very same "harmonious" environment that makes "healthy family interactions" likely.

Promoting open dialogue in the family is a key component of creating a culture of trust and respect. Family meetings or regular check-ins can offer a set time and space for not just saying, but really discussing—together—our core values; for bringing up and, together, navigating any tough issues; and for recognizing and, together, celebrating our various family members' successes. This practice, by which we never let go of the hands of the democratic approach to communication, not only empowers our children to speak up and say what they really think but also to hear and receive what we as parents are thinking.

In the end, family communication was positively affected by practicing gratitude. The familial ties were strengthened, and emotional connections were heightened. Practicing gratitude was a way to render appreciation for even the smallest of acknowledgments. The children began to understand what it meant to be thankful. And expressing thanks became a habit. This allowed for deepening familial bonds and a preservation of family ties. The children learned gratitude, which became an emotional habit that could last for a lifetime.

Approaches to Resolving Disputes

Resolving family disputes is essential if the family is to maintain an environment conducive to the cultivation of its core values. One of the most effective means of doing this is really quite simple: open communications, in which each party in a conflict feels safe expressing himself or herself first and foremost, and ideally without a lot of judgmental interjections from others. It's a given that such a plea for "open conversations" is a simplistic platitude. But the next step, nudging both parties toward real active-listening mode (in which both are somewhat equally engaged in a non-judgmental exchange), is really where the magic happens and is also, I think, where the family truly earns its moniker.

Another effective way is to base modeling and teaching of conflict resolution skills on virtues such as justice and temperance and to involve parents as models of fair assessment in conflicts. Good parents ensure that the viewpoints of all parties in a conflict are heard and considered before a fair resolution that all can accept is reached. Role-playing is a good way to practice this at home. It helps children learn to navigate conflicts in a balanced manner and also provides them with the articulation and negotiating skills that they need to accomplish the same thing as they grow.

Along with communication and skill-building, a culture of empathy can significantly trim the frequency and intensity of family disputes. Teaching family members to recognize and respect one another's emotions can steer the family closer to a state where compassion prevails over conflict. Parents can lead this push by sharing stories that highlight the importance of understanding different perspectives and by using what are almost teachable moments to commend moments when positive resolutions are reached because of—or in spite of—some family member's poor decision or lack of understanding.

A structured family meeting can also serve as an effective way to deal with disputes before they become problematic. These meetings are a time and place to be with family members, to discuss and resolve any issues that may be going unresolved, to set and review expectations, and to recognize achievements that are being made (or have been made) by family members. In fact, I see structured meetings of this nature as a proactive approach to family life and an opportunity for parents to model problem-solving techniques for their children. At the same time, also modeling the idea with these children (and in a without-blame way) that the family unit is best when everyone is pulling in the same direction, has a voice, and is valued.

Finally, it is vital to impart resilience when teaching children conflict resolution. Kids who learn to overcome life's little bumps will have the fortitude to face big challenges when they come. Parents can encourage resilience by framing conflicts as opportunities for growth and learning. When kids are in the middle of a disagreement and they come to a parent for help in resolving it, the first step is to get the kids to reflect on the issue and what they might be able to learn from it. This not only helps in resolving the current disagreement but also sets the kids up to manage future conflicts.

The Lincoln Leadership

Few individuals loom as large as Abraham Lincoln, the 16th President of the United States, in the pages of history. His legacy goes beyond political achievement—yet, even that is momentous in providing a counterpoint to the cruelty of America's founding that the Founding Fathers had attempted to avoid. The cruelty of America's founding is masked in abstract proclamations of liberty. At the same time, the Civil War made Lincoln a martyr, and his wise and sensible way of achieving political ends made him a great leader.

The leadership of Lincoln is at the heart of the stoic principle of prudence, which is defined as the exercise of wise and thoughtful judgment. He was confronted with the worn-torn pressures of a nation. He had to deal with the moral quandaries surrounding slavery. And he had to pacify a cabinet that was rife with dissent. Yet, through all this, Lincoln maintained the stoic ideal of keeping calm and collected in troubled times. And more than that, he modelled for us how to make decisions that do not just react to the immediate chaos of the moment but instead aim to reestablish unity in the nation and maintain it in the long term.

Lincoln's conflict resolution strategy had at its core an understanding of communication—not merely as a means of getting people to do what one wanted them to do but as a necessary ingredient in the development of genuine dialogue that might lead to the resolution of conflicts. If one wanted to get to the resolution of an impasse, one not only had to be good at persuading people but also had to be good at fostering listening on the part of one's audience. And listening, in Lincoln's book, was not just for the audience to hear the words being spoken. Listening, in this context, was appreciating the idea that "Bob, you may have a point to make that I don't understand" or "Bob, I understand you do have some concerns."

Lincoln's Civil War conflict resolution reached its zenith, external and internal hostilities. The Gettysburg Address serves as a profound illustration of Lincoln's philosophical stance. In it, he reframed the war as not merely a confrontation between North and South but as a test of the nation itself. It was a test of whether the nation's foundational ideals could hold together in the face of adversity. Those ideals, stated and restated in both solemn and soaring fashion since the Puritan-communalist enclaves of the 1620s, in the Mayflower Compact, and Winthrop's "A City upon a Hill" speech, and then in the liturgical promises of the American Revolution, had achieved a secular, constitutional form.

The leadership of Lincoln was tied to the stoic virtues of prudence and patience. They are integral to his persona. Wisdom often lies in not acting, and Lincoln had that kind of wisdom. When the country was asking for aggressive action against the Confederacy, Lincoln was stolidly not doing something. Hasty decisions lead to needless suffering, he seemed to know, and even if the country was going to be divided, he was working for a resolution that not unnecessarily hasty action might realize. The patience of stoicism ties Lincoln's leadership to conflict resolution.

Lincoln's philosophy can be seen in his assertion, "I am slow to listen, and quick to act." This underscores the value of emotional control, a vital quality for any leader navigating the pressures of wartime. His ability to exercise restraint is a reminder that the most prudent course of action often involves reflection and contemplation before plunging helm first into decisive measures. Indeed, Lincoln often found himself in the boat of the contemplative leader.

The conflict resolution legacy that Lincoln left is significant. It matters. It is something we can and should learn from. What makes Lincoln's legacy in conflict resolution so powerful is not just what he did but also what he did when confronted with conflict (particularly in the Civil War). Lincoln is famous for virtuous engagement. Virtue is not synonymous with avoidance. Engaging conflict in a virtuous manner is to engage with wisdom, empathy, and respect for differing viewpoints.

Parents can mine Lincoln's methods for valuable, timeless lessons in dealing with family disputes. For Lincoln, resolution of conflict required two things: patience and a mustering of the "stupid" virtues (i.e., virtues that paid off in a big way for him). The virtues of these two things made Lincoln a "good father." And we are here reminded that in these tough times that we face as a nation, it will help to be patient and to exhibit virtues during the necessary conflicts that we must resolve to be a "united" family.

The Role of Prudence in Conflict

Conflict resolution in the family context requires a calm and steady hand and, most importantly, a sense of parental prudence.

VIRTUOUS CONFLICT RESOLUTION

Prudence is kind of a boring word, but it means something really important: You think before you act. And oh, how you should think if you are attempting to resolve a family conflict! You have to consider not only the immediate situation but also the kind of resolution that will be best for everyone involved in the long haul. You have to weigh the needs and emotions of all family members who are in the line of fire. You have to shop around in your mind for a good resolution instead of a quick one and, again, instead of one that might make forceful sense but isn't really all that peaceful or kind.

Prudence, in the context of balanced discipline, encourages parents to choose methods of discipline that are fair and just, with a deep understanding of the child's perspective and emotions. It is all too easy for parents to react impulsively out of frustration or anger and to choose methods that lack the tempering qualities of justice and guidance. What requires much more effort on a parent's part is choosing, in a Sartrean sense, the kind of disciplinary method that is more about teaching and guiding a child than it is about punishing him or her. Prudence counsels against impulsive and poorly thought-out choices.

Another main area in which the prudence of family dynamics expresses itself is emotional intelligence. Families can cultivate a culture of emotional intelligence by communicating openly and promoting emotional awareness. When parents and children understand one another on an emotional level, they can resolve conflicts more easily and naturally. When parents are serious about resolving family conflict and helping their children learn how to do so as well, they listen actively to what their children have to say and validate the children's feelings. This creates a climate of safety where all voices can be heard and where family members know that their feelings are significant.

Ensuring that children grow up to be resilient requires parents to practice another virtue: prudence, especially in conflict situations. When parents approach conflicts with a prudent mindset, they model for their children how to face challenges thoughtfully and constructively. This kind of modeling is essential because children internalize their parents' ways of being. Setbacks, when taken in the right way, are opportunities for learning and growth. Consider two hypothetical situations, one in which a mother leads with reflection and careful decision-making and another in which she doesn't.

In the end, building a family culture around core virtues means being prudent in all interactions, especially when we are tempted to be less than civil in our dealings with one another. Integrating prudence into the virtue practice of family life is a "no-brainer." At some point, every family must consider the age-old question that parents from time immemorial have asked: Is our family a good family? This question can only be asked cerebrally, or in a way that is almost cerebral, if the virtues around which the family is built and the vices that the family avoids are at least somewhat known to family members.

Seven

Cultivating Gratitude

"Not only is gratitude the greatest of virtues; it is the parent of all the others." Cicero

Gratitude stands as a foundational virtue, shaping the very essence of our character and the quality of our relationships. In recognizing the gifts life offers, we cultivate an attitude that fosters resilience and fortitude. When we express gratitude, we acknowledge the interconnectedness of our existence with others and the world around us.

This appreciation serves as a catalyst for the development of other virtues. Wisdom is sharpened as we reflect on the contributions and sacrifices of those who came before us. Courage is emboldened when we recognize the strength drawn from support and shared experiences. Justice is magnified as we become aware of our obligations to others, driving us to act fairly and compassionately.

In the practice of gratitude, we find a powerful antidote to the discontent that arises from envy or resentment. By focusing on what we have rather than what we lack, we align ourselves with the Stoic principle of accepting our circumstances with equanimity. This mindset allows us to remain grounded in our values, even amidst life's challenges.

Furthermore, gratitude nurtures humility, reminding us that we are not solitary beings but part of a larger tapestry of humanity. It encourages us to recognize the roles others play in our journey, fostering deeper connections and promoting a sense of community. In this way, gratitude is not merely an emotion; it is a deliberate choice that influences our actions and interactions.

To cultivate gratitude is to practice the very essence of Stoicism. It invites us to shift our focus from what we cannot control to what we can appreciate. Each day presents opportunities to acknowledge the small and large blessings that enrich our lives. In doing so, we not only elevate our own spirits but also inspire those around us to embrace the same perspective.

As we integrate gratitude into our daily practice, we begin to see it as a foundational virtue that supports the edifice of our character. It shapes our thoughts and actions, guiding us toward a life of purpose and fulfillment. Ultimately, by cultivating gratitude, we lay the groundwork for a virtuous life, where every interaction becomes an opportunity for growth, connection, and understanding. Through this lens, we can truly embrace the wisdom of Cicero, recognizing that gratitude is indeed the parent of all virtues.

In a familial setting, nurturing gratitude can lead to a marked improvement in the mental health of individual members and the collective family unit. To express gratitude, one must recognize and appreciate the contributions of others. The simple act of saying "thank you" can create a ripple effect of positivity, leading to an atmosphere in which all members feel secure, valued, and more closely bonded.

From a stoic perspective, gratitude aligns with the principles of acceptance and focus on what is within our control. Stoicism teaches that we should appreciate what we have rather than obsess over what we don't. This makes it more likely that we will avoid the bad family habit of not acknowledging each other's efforts and simply appreciating one another. If we can't recognize the richness in our relationships, how will we be able to effectively navigate any challenges that may arise?

Gratitude and stoicism within the family can lead to a more harmonious environment in which members support one another. Recognizing and appreciating each other's strengths and efforts is a step toward forming a culture of familial gratitude. Such a culture fosters the conditions necessary for personal and collective growth, balanced by the virtues of the stoic mindset.

The Importance of Gratitude in Family Life

The role gratitude plays within the family is profoundly significant. In a world that seems ever-more focused on material wealth and is held up by an economy of speed, taking time to be grateful for what one has seems almost countercultural. And yet, that's just what some families do: take time to express their thanks for one another and for the kindnesses that family members bestow upon one another in the course of daily life. While there is no compulsory script for expressing thanks within families, the kind of gratitude that one family member can model for another surely sets up an expectation that enhances the familial atmosphere.

Emotional intelligence develops when children express gratitude and appreciation for what they have and for the efforts of others. This is because the act of appreciating is an act of cognition as well as an act of emotion. When children learn to express gratitude with regularity, they are also learning to be more in tune with the thoughts and feelings of people around them. And this is precisely the kind of practice that enhances empathy development, which lays down the foundation for emotionally intelligent navigation through difficult social situations for the rest of a child's life. Parents can encourage the express-through-multiplicity pathway of gratitude development by asking children to list at least three things they are grateful for on a regular basis.

Gratitude serves as a powerful resilience-building tool. When children focus on what they appreciate, it helps them build a resilient way of living. They learn to take what could be seen as a setback or a no-growth place and turn it into an opportunity to grow and maybe even flourish. When families acknowledge and celebrate even the small victories that they might achieve during any given day, when they thank and appreciate each other for simply being there, they create a context where resilience is much more likely to take root.

In addition, nurturing gratitude in a family dovetails nicely with the principles of balanced discipline. When parents focus on fostering gratitude in their children, they set the stage for an understanding that actions have consequences. This consequence knowledge is about justice; the understanding that what was done to another person, whether good or bad, was done in the presence of that person's mind and heart. When parents set the stage for gratitude, they are also helping their children understand the reasonable workings of good and bad "influence."

Ultimately, nurturing a culture of gratitude turns the family setting into one marked by mutual respect and good will. When families make gratitude a priority, they develop an atmosphere in which all members feel valued and are understood. This atmosphere enhances the personal relationships that all family members have with one another. It also serves as a model for children who, having seen and felt the kind of relationships that a family built on gratitude has, are likely to be the kind of "friends for life" and future partners that anyone would want.

Viktor Frankl and the Stoic Pursuit of Meaning Through Gratitude

An Austrian psychiatrist, a Holocaust survivor, and the father of logotherapy, Viktor Frankl shares a potent lesson with us: Gratitude can turn the most intense and bitter adversity into something manageable. Frankl's accounts of his life in the concentration camps, interspersed with teachings from his deep well of psychological knowledge, sends us home with a truth that may feel uncomfortable but also shines with the light of clear wisdom. His text, Man's Search for Meaning, shows us how to reach way down in ourselves until we find the peace that allows us to keep marching forward, even when the path seems to disappear into the dark night of a soul.

What Frankl recounts stands as a stellar tribute to the power of gratitude to serve as a tool for resilience and personal transformation. Even in the most abominable conditions, he saw that those who could forestall despair and somehow find even the slightest hint of meaning in their lives—via thrown-together pastimes of goodness, divine meditation, or fantasy lifeworlds—were not only surviving but emerging from leurs souffrances as humans who had been fundamentally altered and, in many instances, improved.

One of his most stirring pronouncements, Frankl's declaration makes clear a basic tenet of his thinking: no matter how bleak the world appears, we at least possess the power to determine the tenor of our personal response. "We who lived in concentration camps can remember the men who walked through the huts, comforting others, giving away their last piece of bread," he writes, going on to assert that what these pitiable few achieved in the way of right action should serve as proof—if not as a model—for us to do likewise when we find ourselves faced with the kind of impossible choice that would make us lean toward gratitude instead of complaint.

Logotherapy, the philosophy of Frankl, is grounded in the premise that achieving life's meaning comes from something greater than oneself—be it work, love, or spiritual faith. In Frankl's eyes, life is not best approached as a puzzle with all its pieces just waiting to be fit together in a certain way for a person to feel fulfilled. Instead, he sees gratitude as the cognitive bridge leading many people to the kind of "aha!" moment that makes everything else in their lives click.

For Frankl, gratitude was more than just saying "thank you." It was a fundamental attitude toward life and a path he recommended for his fellow prisoners in the Nazi concentration camps. Even when our circumstances are dire, he argued, we can find something to be grateful for—a lesson we can sometimes strive to learn, he acknowledged, only with great difficulty. Life is meaningful, he said, because even the most miserable existence can be made bearable if we find some purpose in it. And what better purpose can there be than to dig deep into our souls and cultivate what he believed to be the most potent of all human virtues: gratitude?

This deep lesson in resilience through gratitude became the cornerstone of Frankl's post-war work. When he returned to his psychiatric practice, he brought with him the lesson he had learned in the concentration camp: the ability to find meaning in life is the most potent ingredient for not just being well but for being mentally and spiritually healthy. For him, not merely existing but living with profound meaning was essential. And for that, he believed, gratitude was key. It was gratitude that allowed one to embrace the moment, to understand the value of love and friendship, and to keep the flame of hope alive.

Frankl's ideas about gratitude infiltrate family life in profoundly and positively transformative ways. Families facing trials of any sort—economic, psychological, or social—can find motivation in Frankl's ability to plumb gratitude from the depths of despair. They can certainly be spurred in that direction by his directing gaze toward the topsails of life. But it is also true that we need to see life as containing enough good to make our grip on it worthwhile. Seeing life's numerous nuggets of gold can nourish our gratitude just as much, if not more, than simply bearing with life's slings and arrows.

Say, for example, that a family suffers a setback—a financial crisis, say, or a health concern. Then what? Frankl's approach would say they ought to focus on what they still have. And what is that? The love that unites them, the health they still possess, the support that binds them together, the wisdom they've gleaned from past struggles, and the peace that's been granted (and generally speaking, the peace that has to be granted) that's almost an unspoken part of any family life when we're collectively under siege.

Frankl's steadfast and tireless ability to promote and elevate gratitude to a position of very high esteem in the realm of psychology and human relations makes him a figure of transformative power for many a family unit in this world, especially in times of great difficulty.

Gratitude is a habit of the heart that can be learned and that can lead to the flourishing of not just individuals but whole families.

—Esther Frankl, in a tribute to her late husband, Viktor Frankl

This story offers an illustration of how gratitude goes beyond just being an emotion; it becomes a path to resilience and virtue. It shows that even in the most unyielding of situations, gratitude can be a game changer in family life.

Practical Ways to Foster Gratitude

It is immensely important to harbor gratitude within a family. Conversely, the benefit of having a family member engaged in expressing gratitude is significant, too. Studies demonstrate that expressing gratitude enhances the virtues of prudence and temperance, not only in the person thanking but also in the recipient. It goes without saying that two or more people expressing gratitude to one another is a good thing. Hearing "thank you" reinforces and strengthens the bond that exists between family members. And when it is done regularly, both in private and, at times, in public, it becomes a habit that is hard to break.

An alternative, equally effective method to nurture gratitude in children is through the celebration of storytelling. Families can come together to tell one another personal stories about times when they were granted help, support, or kindness by others. The storytelling can include some reflections on how those experiences made them feel and the significance of recognizing and acknowledging the contributions made by others that allowed them to live with a semblance of normalcy. By promoting this practice, children learn to appreciate their own blessings, but also the role that community and relationships play in the well-being of their lives. This practice also allows an expansion of the emotional vocabulary—the use of more than just "good" or "bad" in reflecting on experiences—that is so important in developing a strong foundation of emotional intelligence.

Instilling gratitude in children can occur through the effective method of having them write thank-you notes. Be it for gifts received, acts of kindness, or simple gestures, the younger set might need a little extra motivation when it comes to this seemingly antique custom. But it's a great way to encourage emotional expression and clear communication, which are both important virtues in our digitally distracted age.

Phrases that once were a given in good manners—"Thanks," "Thank you," and most importantly, "You're welcome"—seem increasingly rare as we navigate virtual spaces.

Integrating thankfulness into everyday routines can further cultivate this character trait within the family culture. Thankfulness can be modeled by the parents who express thanks for the daily, ordinary, shared experiences that make up family life—enjoying a meal together, admiring a clean home, or savoring recently completed tasks—that could easily go unappreciated. Silence can be a part of thankfulness too. Parents and children can fold moments of appreciative silence into the family culture, culminating in a weekly gathering in which each family member shares one or more occasions for gratitude experienced in the last week.

Finally, providing instruction to children about the influence of thankfulness on mental health and resilience has the potential to be transformative. Parents can talk with their kids about studies demonstrating how a disposition of gratitude relates to enhanced joy and better management of life's difficulties. By promoting gratitude as a means of achieving greater emotional strength, parents position their children to see the good in their lives—to recognize that their family, even in tough times, is virtuous—and to understand that this protective factor against adversity has something to do with the golden rule.

Gratitude as a Pathway to Virtue

Cultivating gratitude is not merely an exercise in politeness; it is the cornerstone of a virtuous life. Gratitude, when nurtured within the family unit, serves as a profound catalyst for resilience. It transcends the fleeting moments of thanks and embeds itself into the very fabric of our character. When parents instill this mindset in their children, they are not just fostering emotional intelligence; they are laying the groundwork for a life anchored in virtue.

This way of thinking, rooted in gratitude, rewires the brain. Children who adopt this perspective become more attuned to the virtues of generosity, kindness, and empathy. The neural pathways that support these qualities strengthen over time, resulting in a more dependable and robust character. It is through the practice of gratitude that the seeds of resilience are sown, allowing individuals to navigate the challenges of life with a steadfast spirit.

Integrating gratitude into daily family routines need not be complex. Simple expressions of thanks during mealtime can initiate this transformative practice. Such moments create a space for reflection and acknowledgment, fostering a collective appreciation for what is shared. Some families elevate this practice into rituals, each unique and infused with joy. These rituals are not burdensome obligations; they are opportunities for connection and celebration of life's blessings.

In observing these family traditions, it becomes clear that joy is a common thread. The act of expressing gratitude is not shrouded in solemnity but rather embraced with lightness and laughter. Furthermore, the presence of a leader in these rituals highlights the sincerity that underpins such practices. This leadership, whether intentional or spontaneous, reflects an authentic appreciation that resonates throughout the family.

Ultimately, gratitude is a pathway to virtue, and through its cultivation, families empower their children to face life with resilience and integrity. In the simplicity of thankfulness, profound lessons await, guiding the next generation toward a life well-lived.

Final Thoughts

Our family life changed forever in 2021. When our son was diagnosed with Sensory Processing Disorder, it felt like the world shifted on its axis. Suddenly, the things we once took for granted—loud noises, textures, transitions, crowded places—became hurdles to navigate with care. But more than that, we began to see the world through his eyes, and in doing so, we were changed too.

Parenting a child with sensory needs has taught me more about virtue than any book ever could. Patience, temperance, courage, compassion—these aren't abstract ideals for us. They're daily practices. They're the quiet decisions made in moments of chaos: when a meltdown begins and I choose to sit beside him instead of trying to stop it; when I slow down long enough to understand the root of his overwhelm instead of reacting to the surface behavior.

Instilling virtue in our home isn't about perfection. It's about modeling how to rise after we fall, how to apologize when we get it wrong, how to listen, and how to love deeply even when it's hard. My children don't need me to be flawless—they need me to be present. They need to see what integrity looks like when no one's watching, what kindness feels like when they're struggling, and what courage means when change comes knocking.

There are days that stretch me in every direction—between work, exhaustion, and the unpredictability that comes with raising a neurodivergent child. But even in the mess of it all, I've found something steady: a deep belief that virtue isn't just taught—it's lived. And I want my children to grow up in a home where that's not just something we talk about, but something they see in action, every day.

This book began as a way to process our journey—but it became something more. It's a reflection of who we are becoming as a family. Not just navigating sensory needs, but building a home grounded in values that will shape our children long after they've grown. A home where love is patient, discipline is fair, and where we remind each other—gently, and often—that who we are becoming matters more than how easy the day has been.

Thank you for walking this road with me. I hope this book finds you at a moment when you, too, are planting seeds of virtue in your own home.

With gratitude,
Phillip Deam

www.ingramcontent.com/pod-product-compliance
Lightning Source LLC
Chambersburg PA
CBHW061751070526
44585CB00025B/2860